Tear in the Cloud

Our Wishing Wells

Nash Sims

iUniverse

TEAR IN THE CLOUD
OUR WISHING WELLS

iUniverse books may be ordered through booksellers or by contacting:

iUniverse
1663 Liberty Drive
Bloomington, IN 47403
www.iuniverse.com
1-800-Authors (1-800-288-4677)

ISBN: 978-1-5320-8866-7 (sc)
ISBN: 978-1-5320-8867-4 (e)

Library of Congress Control Number: 2019919508

Print information available on the last page.

iUniverse rev. date: 11/14/2019

Contents

Prayerful

Said a pray from across town
It had already bet me there and touched down.
The whole comfortness had spread all around
And wouldn't come down from the ground…up.
I bring cheer and happiness to your doorstep,
Fill you city…up.
It's a pity but,
People don't know how much power of a prayer
Across the world touched. A prayer says a lot.
Pray for others first even if not praying for me.
Felt so grateful
Prayerfully pray it's all in me
To do the best I can be all in me
My prayer shed light on the land that was government ran
They don't understand, but you do on the other hand.
Know you can reach my fellow man
Pray for energy receive it instaneously
Butterflies in my gut,
Pray for the pain for the rain and the rainbow
When it clears up.

Say prayers for me and others
Still have love for my sisters and brothers
The way Jehovah loves us can't help but to touch us.
Let him show you. Praying for your problems over mine
And I don't even know tou.
Pray long enough and it will be fixed during his time.
Pray cause he let me shine.

Freedom of choice pray for the birds voice
Pray for me to know for our love grow.
Pray for the oceans current and the flow .
Pray for your will to be done
Pray for your kingdom to come
Under the gorgeous sun
In the name of your son
Pray for the words that sits on my tongue
And the air that hits my lungs and then some
Until my end comes, Father please listen to this one.
Pray to you cause you love me.
Pray that you're the only that can judge me.
There's no one above thee,
Pray for the world despite the wickedness
It's still so lovely.

Aquatic

Escape to the aquatic
Come up for a breath of fresh air periodic
Moonbeams and shadows on the water share
Trying to follow footsteps over there
On the sand but it's a few pair to follow (Ha ha)
They tried that's, cute, try it again tomorrow
(same station) at the aquatic.

Look forward to this underwater vacation
Peace for the duration of our journey
Rode on the fins of a dolphin eager
To do flips and tricks (Ha ha)
Maybe two more
Humble like I was (Four) again
Eager to see what's in store, show me more.
From the top the stillness of the oceans floor
Shore to shore.
Simply just adore getting away
Probably most definitely wanna stay.
Feel the world to do without me.
For a day or so N.E. way
Let go of all my troubles
It's just me and my bubbles
A school of fish I seen a couple
Tickling my wrist
Every time I'm in the aquatic.
Since I've been away from a society that robotic
Been spending all my time at the aquatic
(Peace brothers) Body souls spirit and never watch the time

Your should see how the moonlight shine.
Under water, nobody here to bother me.
The current is who I'm here with.
Take a few breaths on my peace breaths.
On my peace quest too excited to rest.
Side by side animal who's carefree and blessed.
Here at the aquatic nobody hears robotic
My last memories before I left
Is the worlds on big mess
Everybody's stressed
Here I'm more than fresh
Here at the aquatic
Came for peace and peace I got
the aquatic.

Thoughts of U, Thoughts of Me

My thoughts of repetiton
Care to join me on this exhibition
One plus one I'm good at addtion
Visions of being swept away.
And love struck call a physician.
Check me out you have my permission
He discovered uncovered feelings,
Needed someone to share with
Full of color now used to be transparent.
I know your heart
Thoughts of you and thoughts me
Carved A heart in the nearest tree of our initials
I hunger for your love Im starved
Can't describe the craving but it's amazing
Thoughts of me thoughts of you
Who knew oh what to do
Hope your thoughts of me
Is pleasant as can be
Fulling every virtual fantasy
From the T.I.M.E you
W.A.K.E --- U.P.
If my world doesn't consist of you and it's your duty
Please remove me at your leisure
You're a keeper a double feature
Glad to meet ya
Let's dig deep
For whatever been hid

School Crush

Went to sleep thinking deep
Didn't really eat to excited
Head rush thinking about my
School Crush
To cum up with the perfect words
keep me woke, hearts around my love notes in class
Before the teacher threw them in the trash
You laugh, I'm serious
The teacher is furious, probably curious
Take it, read it to her signicate other, softly
Wasn't hearing nothing the teacher said
Way to go, I know. (I know).

Tap my neighbor I know your arms is getting tired
From passing notes but N.E. way, my note said,
Would you like to go out with me, yes or no?
I could do this all day.
Kan I have a kiss in the hall way
Got a crush on you in a tall way
Walk through the hall holdin hands
In front of you all,
Do you like to dance?
Are you willing to take a chance?
(Oh here come the teacher)
Trying to crumble up my note
But the words still stuck in my throat
Can't wait to see you after 3rd
Despite what N.E. body else heard.

Peace

Head between my hands
Focus with all my might
Concentrate hard as I can
Hope my prayers
Expend to all man to every land
Back swamp grain of sand
May these prayers these thoughts
Be heard night and day to night (Peace)

Use profanity to describe the insanity
May you find these words find my brothers and sisters
And illuminate your rights
Or someone else light less bright
Jehovah in the name of Jesus like my mother
Losing her sight, you still got your family
Thanks to yourself (Peace)

Soon as I lose sight soon as I lose my grips on life
With life feel like there's no fight like-------
Soon all I feel tense
I walk where the sky's leave footprints
I think (Peace)
So therefore there is (peace) peace
Life's name I call her cherish and I'm it's Prince
Peace let your imagination free
Let's all meet hold hands every race
Every states everyone and everything that breaths
No one with power except for one and his Son Father cause
Nobody down here is no better than me.

When will they see we're all equal
Those under the weather may my prayers
Be with you forever (peace)

Morning my fellow man we are all the same complextion
Headed in the same direction yes we can
We all made different but the same
Different lanes but same veins
Same pains I imagine
He reigns instead of my shackles and chains (peace)

The word to help me fight the battles
That seem to unravel
Same issues just a time travel
To sky scrapers too gravel
I'll find a place in the sky
To build my castle
Knocked down scarred and bruised
Zombodie from the sideline hollered (peace)

Thought about it hopped back on my saddle
With the grin the stranger knew as if he'd
Knew I'd win I yelled back to him (peace)

Seen some homeless people on the streets
Gave what I could shook his hand and said
(Peace) from inside within
In front of you when you drive or on the side
Maybe its them whose life ain't going right (peace)
Going and coming (peace)
To the kids of the daughters or
The sons who can't be with the mother or daughter (peace)
They still young I could go on and on I wish I had more lungs
(Breath-----------------------Exhale).

(Peace)
I don't need one day to Feast every day is Thanksgiving
Having money ain't living found the jones in the giving
Faith in my Father
(judging not our place)
Think peace so everything around me is (peace)
Please according to my heart rythym
I can send people peace long distance
Keep asking (you know what they say)
And I'm persistant pray for peace for mothers
My sisters and brothers myself every day.

Friend

You are the wind beneath my sails
Anchor holding up my scales
Together we shall prevail
Together or separated I wish you well
Love to kiss and tell
Being here with you I call that
Living well before I could never
Tell infatuations
For all your others I'm gonna
Demand evacuation
You deserve a good man
On her own to is how she stand
From here and beyond is the plan
Just you and me and space that's three
Gliding over the meadows now that's free
Along the way grabbing a couple of peddles over
As the leaves and peddles settle over
Meadows and the sunset having fun yet
I'm on cloud 9 plus ten
Just me and my friend
What we can't fix well let time nmend my
Friend till the time end
Perfect timing lately, you've
Been reminding me of an angel
Can't nobody ever step into our rectangle

Space and You

Escape the subconscious
Crates with our love snacks for
Our picnics in our napsacks
Nothing but our sits and starmaps
Like star track
Falling stars to your left something to gaze at
You handle this trip exceptionally
Was going to make a wish, but I already got
My star right here sitting next to me
Set to speeds incredibly
Thinking to myself your made with all things nice
And asking your mother for the receipe
Stars ran into cluster
Space is nice but nothing like when I touch ya
Forgot for a second that I was traveling
Done a lot tof things but your something I'd like to dabble in
The odometer reads E.T.A. possible a light year
Just as long as I got you
I'll be right here
Kick off our shoes seems a though we'll be here for a few
Doesn't matter if we take it fast or slow
Brain stll trying to take in all the data
Throw a star watch em scatter
Space trip greener pastures
That last for (pause) (A -----while)
Looking at the essence
Of life love to share it
Within your presence no need for-----exits.

Do as I do breathe hard on the window
Imaginations
Out of this
World twirl
Like it's rotations
Till we reach the
\ Hole in space in and
Beyond to see where the roads
Takes in
We await our path
No gas
Imagination fuels the aircraft
That last beyond the vast
So fast as though a flash
Stars and quasars on the maze
Lights threw the night pierce the
Darkness like (lassers)
Trip is outstanding regardless
Cheers to a safe landing

Companion

Unwhole when you're absent
Time seems to drag, draydream just to help me
Pass it no longer search for peace of mind
Crazy glue to help me patch it
Keep it together like 2 shoes
With that spectacular magic that you do
2 true definitely somebody to hold on to

Gathering my words right before you walk through the door
Words and works of understanding I truly adore
The good and bad days don't necessarily have to be
One day just thought I'd take a little time out to say

Thanks for being a companion (thanks for the understanding)
Hold them close hell have a toast
Make some love make love to each other's mind
Just unwind and enjoy the time
That's what really means the most

Head to the moon let the stars chase us
Hold hands*** leap into the future
See where it takes us to let the world embrace us
We're going places tie your laces
Ready for the future and the present
Your heart is protected.

Tear in the Cloud

Tear in the cloud
Look it's there right now (it's there right now)
Looks as though there was a big zipper zipped down
I'm trying my best to get closer
I'd snap a shot or two
Put it on a poster
Zip it up zip it down when it rains
Zip it up zip it down
Watch the weather change
Watch a rainbow from the horizon
From where I stay to where I see
The giant zipper everyday this particular
Cloud to me is exciting
It's as though somebody hiding behind the cloud
Bet I'd yell my thoughts to the heavens
Cause my Gods never hiding
Thought I seen a giant finger unzipping the cloud
While I was driving

Ponderosa

Who's the stranger approaches over the ponderosa
Catch you in the middle of your dance
Glance over your shoulder tilt my brim
Me and you equal two tens
Twist and twirl as if we'd be the only ones in the world
But in front of all the jealous men's
And they friend of the friends
Dress blowing step off my steed
Drop the reigns catch your scarf in the winds
Gust blow wind chimes tango
By the saloon of beers and
Whiz where everybody in winds sometimes
Waiting to hear word about the gold mines
She glides smooth as her words
While I'm thinking to myself love is for the birds
Mumbled to myself under my singing
Old timer next to me drinking
I know what he was thinking
One hand on her hip the
Other on my holster
Whispering to me I even look
Handsome on my wanted posters
She pulls me closer
Wondering if what's poking her
In her side was my gun and holster
Probably want me to show her.

Beside Me

Life was so hard I didn't know what to do,
Then I prayed to God, and He sent me to you
And know the world is so beautiful and so grand,
Because you're beside me always and forever,
Holding my hand.

I'll always love you

Intertwine

Anger, will be overcome by your laughter
Shortly after hand in greener pastures
I'm impatient wish we could get their faster
But the chain reaction could and would spell
(Disaster)
Disaster should be avoided if possible?
Don't mind taking our time, jumping through hoops,
Hurdles and obstacles, mutual grounds that's practical
And logical in our quest of
Leaping tall bounds drown in the quick sands of
Companions land with nothing but beauty, to and
Fro and love all around
Once was lost, but now we're found
Star bound star struck the just lost out
With having you tuff luck.

Mines now, this I vow
Time to slip by I won't allow
Let our minds intertwine
Something so divine
You and I

Come Closer

Ever been next to somebody, and your
Heart beats quicker, and you get rushes
Seems as though these mere words, and this
Paper, don't do justice, plus it's
Just not enough time in a day,
To say what I got to say
Feel there's too much space in between us
Wouldn't want to let the time slip through my fingers
Still can't describe what you do to me in
A verse or no matter how I choose to word it
According to that calculator in my head,
Our numbers are more than perfect

The electric charge to my circuits
Sand paper to my surface
A part of something somebody
So my time on earth isn't worthless
The best I can relay
These message and if you use these
Methods the time with you is
Worth way more than any presents.

Life Underwater

Gaze into the light mesmerized softly
By a fish tank at night wondering what a fishes
Life would be like, similar to love as husband and
Wife overcoming all of our trouble chasing dreams
Seems as though dreams are bubbles some bubbles has
Gotten away to quickly side to side swimming against
The tides like me and you swimming against the
World could have sworn I seen a pearl but it
Was simply your reflection cast come on lets
Jump in the current it isn't no stopping the ocean
Meaning the World is vast (vast is the (water)
For my journeys and friends until all of the bubbles
For me thank my Heavenly (Father) and my family.
Heart soul and muscles despite our troubles I call it
(fate) because of my (faith) (face) to (face)
While we have the (Space) there's no so thing as (luck)
I want our paths rocky baby we not learning
Nothing on the (short cuts) only our fins
Torn (up) I love the way the bubbles twirl and
Spin like the way you twirl my world.

Day and Nature

Purple violet green lining in a rainbow feel as though
I can touch it as it hangs low
When I jump I feel like as a feather
Baby birds chirping While Mama bird building a nest
Tying together some twigs
Ants study working as they dig a thing of beauty
Covers the gaze and smoothers it's thick fog and
Settle on a creek with two lovers sitting on a log
To excited by the scenery to sleep
Capture that no Kodak
Snap the picture in my head now hold that say cheese
Driven like children flying kites in the breeze by threes
Dance and float on the trees about 60 something degrees
Perfect as the honey from the bees
No wants and needs you may taunt my speech
But it's real to me no dream two dears nosing by the stream
Positive sayings in the clouds that's floating
Smell the scents of the roses near by
The aroma is potent decoded a message in the stars
I got out of was wisdom Jehovah must had to wrote it
Beauty for his children the very thought of it is chilling
If animals could talk they'd say a million
Revealing the satisfaction, I been feeling
Go together like fraction in my world
While the world around me collapsing
This is my net of safety
Love to embrace thee.

Timelapse

Kiss by the meadows
That's the greenest
Candle only thing between us
A kiss will jump start my circuits

Make my pulse and rhythm
Skip by a big percent and division
Put your head to my chest and listen
You're taken away my breath
Collecting your kisses like butterflies
Under perfectly blue skies
Perfect Lives
Ready for what lies
Or awaits us love to fantasize
Eyes on the prize

Stand firm against ups and down
That arise
No matter the size
Soul mates
The Ties that
Bind our kind
Your eyes are so kind
Cherish our time
Can I make love to your mind?

Pulse and Rythym

Excited as two cloud collided rhythm of my pulse
Dangerous from the beauty that much of a dose at once
And survive it
Jump on melodies of birds ride along with the chirps and
Words there goes my pulse again
When heard

Like the pulse of the wind pulse of my lover and friend
Till the end
Combining our rhythm exciting rhythms of the rain
Thunder and Lighting
Pulse rhythm of the swimming creatures down under
Rhythm of the stars and quasar
To many to number

As long as breathe the knowledge I hunger
Summer to Summer
Talk to plants and animals they have pulses and rhythms
Just listen
Bet they sit and wonder ponder fruitfulness
Is bliss so on and so forth down the list
Makes my pulse that much stronger last that much longer
Secretly or public
It's a rhythm of pulse like me
We're family soon as I touch it
Got to love it.

Massage Therapy

Sometime the worlds unbearable
My mind can't unwind
When it came time probably just needed a little
Massage therapy
The perfect potion for heated oils and scented lotions
Stretch out to an upward motion steady coasting
On a bed still feel like your floating
Baby oil on your body just soaking jazz knocking
Forget about your worries forget about your problems

Fixed up thoroughly in massage therapy
Deep into muscles almost putting me to sleep
That's what I needed desperately massage therapy
More than time passive hands of an angel plus attractive

Cloud so I'm floating this moment are golden
Love that heated lotion despite when the times completed
Working out kinks and things here and there pains
From all my day to day aches feeling good now
Please no breaks please right there all in your neck
She deserves a check
So soothing are her words the outside world is for the birds
Coming back second and third times
She helps you unwind ease your mind
Worries are a disease I tell them all to freeze like breeze
Right now I picture trees bee's beaver's seas to seas
Problems leaves see you later
Massage therapy

Your Type

Answer to your question thought of when I'm resting
Absent or present at the present
Beyond our paths that don't seem long
When seen by two people
Faith help overcome the evil by other people
Let's stay focused
Let's be hopeful
Not the hopeless
The world already knows this
That's why they jealous
Can't stop the zealous
Never meant to be that's why they tell us
And sell us

I've been ready for this flight for some time
Night to become day time
That's what your shine brought me this lifetime
Expand my lifeline
Wish they have similar what they saying in their mind
Intertwine like flowers for hours
Together dance under showers
Gaze and glance at the site of romance all night that's right
My Father knows me and you tighter than bows glad it shows
Hope the world and everybody from here to Saturn knows
Make love to your shadows faster than light travels
Inspired to write about your type

Accommodating

Hope my words and actions are not to dominating
Plan to be more accommodating
Help build and strengthen our relation

Ships show you and tell from my lips
Rather show you (I'm supposed to) suppose to
Show her you love her
Some other day may be tougher than other days
Show her in so many ways you'd be amazed
Your dinner was waiting your bath was ran
Bubble baths to candle to match oils by the tub
With the handles massage table ready for the rub
Tonight we staying in and going a dancing at our own club
The D.J. makes you want to just throw your stress away
I'm Just being accommodating
Know you've been stressing this worlds depressing
But me I'll take that right away
Dance the night away time you'll be loving
Go grab the wine by my little instructions
That say pop the cork it's me and you all for one or nothing
The world seems like a prison just needed somebody to listen
Put in my position to help through transitions
Love to watch you from a distance
Your love slave in an instant said it and meant it
Whatever heartaches you have
Let me mend it.

In Touch

Looking in scratching my chin means to an end
Friends gone in the winds some over ends
Greedy it's easy to see it in their actions
And their grins never ends
Depends never co habit together since forever
Some buckled under the pressure
You different from me but we're equal still people
Combative to the evil we're all weak

In the devil's creek we're all knee deep
Just stand tall others will help you so you don't fall
Sisters and Brothers may Jehovah touch us
Avoided life's brushes couldn't see over the weed
To finer pastures my Father brought the tractors
For the weeds it was a disaster
The roof got cut down me and my friend stay in touch now
Thank you so much may you and me always stay in touch
Apologize for all those absent months
When things got when things got too
much and they hit me all at once
Glad now I come to you first trust me
Things could be a lot worse I could have
looked down screwed up dead
Rolling in somebody's hearse
Still can't describe it in the verse got me so excited
The real holy ghost loves it how my friend pulls me close
Helps my hopes deny me nor try me always fair
Unlike my friends in the wind he was always there
It was I that turned my back on him

Our tests is appetites of the fleshless
Leaves your lives restless and breathless
How we are accepting us that's what caught me theirs
No evil bone in your body never knocked me
In touch now N.E. day is good day above ground.

Never Change

Though we've lived and loved each other
Through the ever changing years,
You've never failed to bring me
Such hope, gladness, and cheers.
I never had a day of sorrow,
that was not satisfying to me,
for you put your loving light,
where darkness used to be.
My love for you is endless,
Far beyond my words could say
for you're the one thing in my life
And that I'm always here to stay.

Happy Valentines Day

Nature

Breaze move around the seeds
Tumble weeds sweeps the praire
Sitting under a tree of apples and
cherry oranges and plums
grown from rays of sun freshness
leaves me breathless restless
even though days unwinding defining the
night transitions of stars moon and the
sun switch positions Cosmic exibitions
natures missions I visions to listen to sounds of nature.

Whistle along my qwest - following a rainbow
over the vast earth with the shadows
Cast and stretches winds are brisky dawgs
catching frisbies cats feeling frisky as they
frolic gusts are iffy feel like Im a cloud
and driffting tipsy off life bussin off life,
life Im loving

Suggestions

She blushes such as lifes cluthches
in my arms hold it tight in my palms
rose peddals floats
away on ponds and settles
quiet rivers misty streams magical
moonlight starbeams shine pierces
the watery deep under the stars to
dream of you while I sleep frog on
a leaf watching me take in your
perfume through my nostrils birds sings
gospels other animals follow perfect
couple me and you perfect roll models
uncork my love notes in a bottle swallow
your beauty I was feeling hollow
confident about tommorow, today it gives
me something to think about trails I seen
a route moonlight catches your completion
fire fly's gives me a suggestion to pop
the question in a group collecting a few
to spell out I love you expression from
my intestine leaves collecting under a tree
to many to number while
squirrells slumber

Love Letters

May wherever however my love letters
reach you may the sunlight if its at night
shine upon your back and come and warm
and heat you through a storm hope in
not a burden as I write this your proably sleeping
working wish I had you in my palm
with a tight grip feel like we born
together at the waist or the hips together
so tight so I write whisper your name it
gets stuck up in my wind pipe its been my
delight fantacising of your silahawette and lips
when we kiss you I truly miss forgive me
for the things in the past I didnt understand
fully should have taken better measures learn
how to better cherish my most valuable
treasures material comes and goes but the love
in my heart I send to you in my love letters.

People thinking Im tripping cause every time I get
your letters I take it hold it to my nose
and sniff it laughing out loud kause I
know you have on that perfume I like when
you did it apologise for taking your words
and twist it your laugh and touch I miss
it whatever pain I caused let me try to fix
it communication was the tickett if I could
I would reverse time I would wish it
shouldnt have been a statitik should have been
more realistic think before I go balistic, states away
no matter the height or distance

Heartbeat

My heart keeps beaten on my qwest
for reason pain feels like it deepen
barely leaves me breathing hopefully Im worth
Keeping despite my smoking and drinking at night
got me thinking barely leaning
been thinking about leaving

but Im not a coward
it poured it showered the world the devil
devoured I call him a coward
now or never trying to keep it together
people will push your buttons
without you Im truly nothing
still things I truly dont understand truly, and
proably wont in this lifetime
for the duration of my lifeline

Perfect

She finishes my sentences
replenishes my souls fires with your love
coals heats me up before igniting perfume
appetizing fantacizing in the day time day
dreaming leaning a pole smirking Im certain
She is an angel in person
I get caught up in her web and dangle
she be all in my head with her love
thread got me wrapped up in her web of lust
merely dust cant get enough love to love,

love me back in love with the fact
perhaps or collapse from trying.
In love with holding your hands like
Peter Pan and flying inlove with trying new,
no barriers zip code to zip code
area to area the whole
entire mass
after the sun and moon pass
Ill still be caught up in your web of
desire shooting stars reflecting in her eyeball
howl like wollves over
you at nightfall
feast on your love at day break
with my easel of love
to create
a perfect master piece

Cosmic Lust

Cosmic cluster shoot, gleam in my eyes
flies atmosphere tears of clouds open leave
the land soaken
clusters in your eyes stolen from the galaxy
aradicly, pratically light speed star breed
stars need a beauty with that twinkle gleam
makes me fiend with moon beams flash
visions of love to make it last cast
reflections over lakes so vast of stars Ive been
collecting picky with my selections
sessions in the in the sunlight digesting
sexy like you the warm corress me till the
day breaks.

Words often times its hard for me to muster I
luster over your cosmic cluster
share your galaxy with me please dont make
me suffer
please dont make me wait
I would love to take you out for a date
I was thinking about jumping on a astroid
and skate
slide
Cosmic cluster of lust collide

Magic with a Friend

To be here with you at this particular time on the planet laying
under you in the moonlight here on this hammock your eyes twinkle
your eyes mingle with mines like magpies sings sweet lolibies
sways swings to the wind season to create magic with a friend

Picked these daffodills off the sides of hills not to far away
lillys colour a pathway where a deer and her child lay in reach
of a sunray young boy high school crush carving his girlfriend
name in a tree, handed her a peach must be something in
the wind perfect season to create magic with a friend.

Come join my bubble
soak me with your love
leave me in a big puddle
my princess and Im the prince
shoes off walking in the sand
leaving footprints
walking to the roses I left you on a park
bench posters with I love you from a marker
then I hung on a fence
magic with a friend

Shoot me with your love laser
rose peddals leading to the poems
I left for you on the refrigerator on paper
welcome to the feast of love
and Ill be waiter Im here to serve and
cater craving for your flavor
some of your lips now

some of your lips for later
for me to bask in the moment pause and saivor

Cook lunch for a picnic
gently touch your lips glance at
your lipstick
now its a rainbow early it was raining out
2 glasses
a baskett with a little of the sheet
hanging out
embrace the time and location
worth celebrating
2 dozen rosses Ive been saiving
for you on this joyous occasion
Magic with a friend

Destinees Harp

Melodies in my head
while Im out and about or laying
in my bed
swim through
the currents of chance
destines harp shall we dance
to enhance the
missions between dreams and moonbeams
gleam through my window
stenstil
victory in the mental
others have fallen before us in order
for us to continue
keep seeking
and reaching for reason
for breathing lifes essence
destinees harp
play a melodic
for we are each others
presents

Sea Shells

Listen to some sea shells
see the sea shells tossed a few down
sum deep wells make beautiful basketts
for ladies females details, details listen
to my sea shells

They tell a story I dont have to do any
talking they do it for me washed to the
shore, shortly I would find delight
glowing even at night driven thru the night
by the light thats bright sum all white
sum with stripes I thought that was alright
alright.

Actually more than alright cause it was all
different types to choose from that one this
one pick some pick them all under the
starry weather all in a row scattered but
somewhat lined up together found a few in
deep wells
listen to the sea shells

Sun Rays

Sunsets leaves me inspired beauty has me
wired real life movie
pots of gold how should I pursue thee
breeze rolls over the meadows so
smoothly then over the creek and settles
floating rose peddalls sunsets with its
different levels.
Walk closer rainbows dont seem so distant
my path illuminated by moonbeans
butterflies lie on my shoestrings, yall along
for the ride a few more to each side

By the winding and sleeping creek wana stay
the whole week plus the weekend watching
different kolours at dusk plus one days not
enough love not lust what the bubble I live
in has to offer birds voices get
softer woman swing with her daughter
through the window waiving at her father
schene of wowness for this nowness
tear in the cloud I found its next to
devine here the sun always shine

My Fathers Soldier

I feel like my fathers soldier here on
earth sometimes lifes a.
from the sidelines how I watch her
the world try to smother my soul take
away my straight posture bury me whole
bring down my helicopter.

I say soldier kause despite the quicksand
apparently my future is supposed to reveal
other plans so I grab on these vines
mixed with guidelines found myself quick
inch by inch thangs felt condensed smaller
I felt taller head was no longer underwater
my heart beated stronger.

Im my fathers soldier I cant be defeated
my brother had hate written all ovah
his face kind words is what he needed,
Im on a mission, kaint keep my people
in the distance the mission is assistance
the world of relentless drain you after
its all done and finished
my fathers strength and guidance
for that unbreakable aliance I am
my fathers soldier

Replenish

Never just a hi and by, their lie a creek
where everyone gather to listen to the music
a creek runs thru it between two villages
peaceful now but who once fuded gold and
diamonds fueled it, thing of the past
xcluded.

Finished all creeds of life come to get
replenished after feeling demenished despite
the weather the river brings people together

To come drink and satisfy their thirst mothers
let their young drink first the river runs for
miles and miles people walk along with pik nik
basketts and bring smiles, older generations
speeches and stones before the younger ones
were born, skipping rocks that look like they
took thousands of years to form.

The cloud in the sky was torn together the
people prepare themselves for the storms we
prepared for the rain but it never came.

Star Qwest

We headed to where quazars fling,
kars and the stars, cell phones no bars
navigation so far from this point
I follow star maps the star qwest pass
by stars while they rest sunsets so close
to us will take your breathe, gather up
a couple stars as a momento in the sky
theirs a few left undescribable with a pen
or pencil or any instrumental, steady with a
tempo to any being star qwest journey
is influencial xcellent essentials perfect
potentials for my mentals.

Space craft next to me was a couple I
watch their flame get rekindled others say other
things are devine as this time while I
reclyne, they must have gotten swindled
these clouds are fluffy as cotton with a
mild breeze eye kandy as far as the
eyes can see and beyond 2,000 knotts
heres where I belong space crafts dont
require gas their powered by our thoughts
for hours and hours for things to discover
xposed by the sun as I glows then rotates
to the other side of the globe as it
goes and rose this journey is best left
for the pros

Sandy Beaches

Sittin on sandy beaches
stroll with some xpensive brandy
will do me dandy watch the water as
far as it reaches from shallow to the deepest
parts be among the many with captivated
hearts until the waves crash on the shore
and reveal the oceans secrets it has a right
to be concealed you should see it at night

then again at first light fall in love at
first site caint do anything but to enjoy life,
Man, woman,
water settles
walk barefoot through
sand and pebbles
love is deep like the water
I wanna test it
wanna drown in your love wheres the
life guard when you need him
you left me breathless drowning in your essence
as far as the eyes can see
across the land draw a heart with
my finger and both our initials
in the sand

Anywhere

I belong to the trees water the breaze
Soul free as the leaves
come and go as I please
little in the wind a little spread over
seas no place for me here or there

Yesterday I seen a cloud with a tear while
I sat in a chair without anyone to share
gaze at the world and stare
felt like I didnt belong anywhere

Would love to be sombodies man settle down
start a family
but people seem to have difficulties understanding
me so used to being lonely I dont even
give people a chance to see
Ima be who I was destined to be
loneliness plays over and over in my head while
Im restine
part of my depression again with that same question
stressin off lonliness
the more I think about it the smaller
my circle gets
till I proably dont even fit

Most of the time I caint stand it
always lonely but we beautiful individuals
so why settle or lower our standards

Look different
talk different sometimes a mental prision
where in the only one who seems
to listen
dont like my story or the way I tell it
cause Im scared up bruised up
abused me and my mother
sisters just cause you hate me doesnt
mean Im here for others to suffer
whoever you are you still a king you still
a queens

dont belong any place where you try to
shatter my dreams my journeys seem so
long cause I keep having to get rid of people
and move on
not a follower so where in the world do
I belong
tired of reaching for help
watch sunrises and sunsets by myself
most of the time devastating
I guess for those like me
we just dont meet other people
expectations or how they felt it is what it is I
Still have to love myself

Paradise Silahwette

Leaves cover the streets and smother the
others with different designs and colours
of fire even other streets prior
different aray in long lines
huming birds to greet you when opening window
blinds devines
the aromas mixtures from around the corner
fresh bread baked across the street
old couple sittin on the porch sitting down
but enjoying life even though they often weak
holding hands watching and listening to a bird
speak asking her to dance giving her a glance

leave piles leaves kids even adults in a trance
feeling like a kid
somethings you got to busy to do or make
time for when you got big
cats and kittens feeling frisky
dozen koulours at sunset to compliment
the city
fellowship uplifting
loving each other not in so much of
a hurry but actually stop offer water
if you thirsty
clothes if you dirty
advice and assurement if you worry
free is the price for advice
the atmosphere is nice despite the weather
pick each other up so we can all do
it together it proably, live there forever
flowers couldnt get no fresher singing in the rain when it showers

Printed in the United States
By Bookmasters